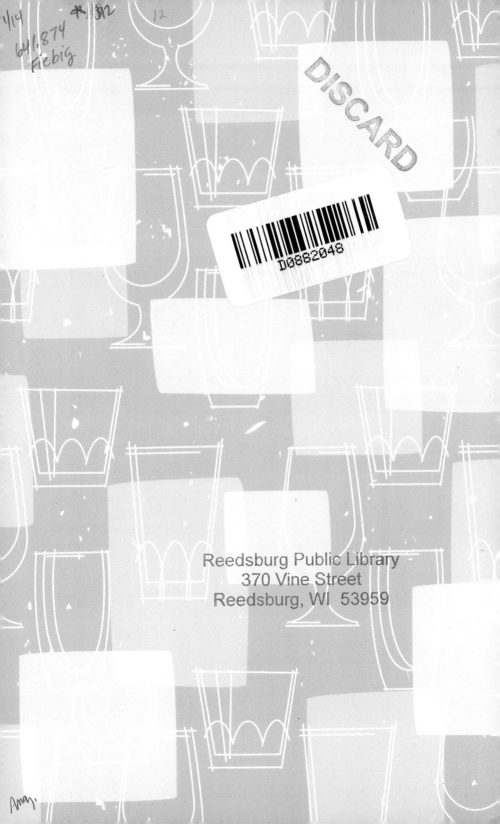

MAY 1959

As you can see in this photograph, Susan (she's the one in the front!) hung out in her grandparents' tavern at an early age. They taught her how to wash bar glasses, wipe the counter, and eventually how to drink . . . responsibly!

She doesn't claim to be an expert when it comes to Bloody Marys. . . . She just knows what she likes, and her choices in this guide represent those Bloodys that are delicious, nutritious, and amazing, in her opinion.

Susan enjoys being on the road, whether in her home state or someplace exotic.

She captures her adventures in her artwork and her writing. Although she is a published author of poetry, this is her first travel guide, and she plans on writing more with help from readers like you!

To learn more about The Bloody Trail, or to contact Susan directly, visit her website at www.thebloodytrail.com.

THE BLOODY TRAIL

BY SUSAN L. FIEBIG

DESIGN & ILLUSTRATION BY
JESSE ROELKE

GRAPHIC DESIGN BY
DIANE MURPHY

Published by Orange Hat Publishing 2013

ISBN 978-1-937165-57-4

www.orangehatpublishing.com

DEDICATION

This book has been my passion since ordering those first Bloody Marys twelve years ago with my dear friend Lindsey. His support and encouragement kept my vision to spread the word about the best Bloodys in Wisconsin alive and kicking!

Whenever I order a Bloody, I will think of you. Cheers!

AUTHOR'S ACKNOWLEDGEMENTS

A special thank you to Jesse Roelke and Diane Murphy, whose extraordinary talents transformed my vision onto paper with skill and enthusiasm. Thank you for bringing my book to life.

Thank you to all of my dear friends, who remained steadfast and believed in me and this book even during the 'dry times'!

Thank you to my family, who love me just the way I am. And to my daughters, who continue to inspire me to pursue my dreams.

THE BLOODY CONTENTS

THE BEST ON THE ROUTE

AND SO IT BEGINS...

On our second date at High Cliff State Park in November of 2001, Lindsey and I naively ordered two Bloody Mary cocktails, unknowingly creating a shared passion that would become known as our GREAT BLOODY MARY QUEST. Several dates and numerous Bloody Marys later, we began rating the drinks, using a scale of one to ten, on cocktail napkins. After four months together, we created a numerical system for greater accuracy.

We developed the Bloody Score to define the system and enable us to maintain some sort of order as we traveled from place to place in the United States and out of the country. During those trips, we always searched for the best Bloody Marys. We learned where to find them by word of mouth from friends and strangers and by reading about them on roadside signs or restaurant menus. Many restaurants were subtle, but some declared they had "The Best Bloody in the World!" Unfortunately, sometimes they were wrong! But on revisits, the same bar would score differently, often as a result of the skills of the bartender. Each drinkologist has his or her own style, and unless the establishment has specific rules as to how to make their Bloody Mary, the taste and style will vary. We are often surprised at the difference! But, all in all, if the drink tastes good, arrives in the right-sized glass, has the proper presentation that includes veggies, and comes with a beer chaser, the score will be a good one!

In our travels, we found that neither the West Coast nor the East Coast really knows what a good Bloody Mary is! Establishments we visited used ingredients that were below average—either too salty or not seasoned enough. They did not know that by adding just one olive and a celery stick, their scores would have been better. The size of the Bloody was also a factor.

What might have been a high-scoring Bloody turned sour when there were NO vegetables in the glass, it was served in a small glass, or it was missing a BEER CHASER! All of these factors are extremely important in order to earn a high score. As you will see, we are merciless.

We have sampled Bloody Marys from Seattle to Santa Fe to SoHo and have determined that Wisconsin, until proven otherwise, is the only state that truly knows how to make a good Bloody Mary! Of course, this varies from bar to bar and restaurant to restaurant, but, overall, Wisconsin knows that veggies are important, the size of the glass is important, and the beer chaser is of UTMOST importance!

This book is certainly the culmination of what we discovered during our travels. We have not tired of tasting Bloodys, and hopefully we never will. We still love the drink and will continue the Bloody Search as long as we can lift the glass to our lips.

Inside this book, you will find the history of each establishment, their "secret ingredients" (if they chose to disclose them), photos of their best Bloody Mary, and a sketch of the place. But most importantly, you will see their scores. Take this book with you as you visit our "Top 10+1 Bloody Marys" and discover for yourself what constitutes a high score.

In addition, the Bloody Challenge invites you to participate in the next edition of The Bloody Trail. Go to www.thebloodytrail.com or mail a postcard to the address at the end of this guide and tell us your favorite Bloody Mary location. We encourage you to keep up the search.

It began innocently enough, but the quest for the best Bloody Mary has grown steadily over time. For us, it's not just about the cocktails . . . it's about spending time together and sharing something unique.

Who knows, the next time you are at the bar drinking a Bloody Mary, we might be sitting beside you! If that be the case, the drinks are on us!

Cheers!

BLOODY HISTORY 101

Although we are not fans of history, a few words should be said regarding the origin of the Bloody Mary. There are many stories claiming to be the real one behind the drink. One includes George Jessel and his friend Mary Geraghty; another describes Ernest Hemingway in Hong Kong in the 1940s and the fall of the Japanese Army; and there's the character named Bloody Mary from James Michener's Tales of the South Pacific (Joseph Scott and Donald Bain, The World's Best Bartender's Guide, HP Books 1998).

But this one works best for me: In the 1920s, Fernand Petiot, a bartender at Harry's New York Bar in Paris, mixed up a concoction of equal parts of vodka and tomato juice. An American patron at the bar called it a Bloody Mary, after a girl he knew from the Bucket of Blood Club in Chicago. The name stuck when Petiot moved to New York City in 1934, became head barman of the King Cole Bar at the St. Regis, and brought his Bloody Mary recipe with him. The hotel wanted Petiot to rename his concoction the Red Snapper, but the name was not popular with the patrons. They also wanted their drinks a bit spicier, so Petiot added black pepper and Worcestershire sauce to his mix and changed the name back to Bloody Mary. It was a success, and everyone was happy!

FERNAND PETIOT

There are many more stories behind the origin of the Bloody Mary and more discussion can be found about Bloody Marys at www.thinkingbartender.com and www.BestBloodyMary.com. Go ahead and do your research if you must, but I am going to enjoy my Bloody regardless of who made it first!

THE BLOODY CRITERIA

 Glass: A simple pint beer glass is preferred.

 Celery Salt: On the rim of the glass.

 Shaken: With the use of a cocktail shaker.

 Veggies: At least 4 are preferred, more is better, variety is crucial.

 Beer: Size is everything.

 Taste: Mix or from scratch, taste is King.

 Presentation: Overall appearance of the delivery.

When judging a Bloody using our criteria, please note that we are generous as long as the Bloody tastes good and the atmosphere is pleasant. The ambience of the establishment can make or break a good score, as does the personality of the bartender. But ultimately it is the drink that gets the final score. A good Bloody can often erase a poor dining experience.

 First, a Bloody should always be served in a tall glass. This is better for overall presentation but also because, if the drink tastes good, we always want more. But we have yet to order a second Bloody, as a good one is usually enough, and a bad one is usually left behind!

 Celery salt is most often added to the mix, but a good Bloody will have celery salt around the rim; the saltier the better!

 A great bartender knows the importance of using a shaker to stir his/her drinks. A great Bloody is ALWAYS stirred or, better yet, shaken. Often, if there is an audience, the bartender will make a spectacle of the procedure and pour one mix into another glass and back again. This always gets the Bloody a higher score.

Now to the veggie score! This is so very important and is unfortunately often overlooked. Even a great-tasting Bloody will not score high if the veggies are scarce. We prefer, at the very least, a pickle, celery stalk, and two olives. Anything less is just not worthy of a good score. The high scorers in this book demonstrate going over the top! Notice how the addition of a sausage stick, string cheese, or shrimp increases the rating. We always say, "A Bloody Mary should be an appetizer to a good meal!"

There has been a resurgence of the Bloody Mary cocktail in local bars and restaurants in the last 5+ years, creating a competition between establishments. Many enterprising owners have added mini-burgers or brats or a thick slice of bacon with the veggie list! BONUS! We always enjoy an appetizer in our Bloodys, and now it is becoming standard procedure.

When it comes to the beer chaser, well, that is always your preference. (It constitutes another book—but there are already plenty of them out there about BEER! We will not even go there!) Sorry, but in this case, size does matter! A beer chaser means two things (at least in Wisconsin): FREE and BIG! For a good score, we demand a 6-ounce beer, at least. It has to look good sitting next to that 12-ounce Bloody Mary. We have seen the cute little beer mugs and miniature beer glasses, and although charming, they just don't add up. Give us a beer that matches the Bloody, or you will score low! This is often the high-score breaker, even with a great-tasting Bloody. And if you cannot give us a free beer, then don't bother at all!

Overall taste of the Bloody cannot be overlooked and will oftentimes make what might be a poor score a bit better. Nothing beats a tasty special mix made right at the bar each night. From experience, we do not get the secret easily, but we have prodded a few from personable bartenders. It could be just adding a bit o' Guinness or Worcestershire sauce that makes a good drink. Clamato juice is often used, especially at seafood restaurants! The most popular ingredient in house mixes is the TABASCO® brand Pepper Sauce by McIlhenny Company. It has been around since 1868 and continues to add a little spice to one's life. One restaurant served a miniature bottle of TABASCO® with each Bloody Mary! Very good move!!! We also love the addition of horseradish to the mix. This gives the Bloody a sassy bite that keeps you on your toes. Spice is nice!

 Now down to the last criteria: overall presentation. All of the above components of a good Bloody make for a high score. Let's review:

1. Large glass—the bigger the better
2. Celery salt rubbed along the rim of the glass.
3. Shaken—preferably with a cocktail shaker.
4. Lots and lots of veggies—throw in a Slim Jim® or shrimp!
5. Beer—big and beautiful, your choice.
6. Taste—spicy and flavorful

There you have it! All of these criteria make for a beautiful presentation. They work together to create the perfect Bloody Mary ... or at least a high-scoring one.

THE BLOODY SCORE

A word on consistency . . . don't hold us to the score if the bartender is having a bad day or if a different or even new (just graduated from mixology college) bartender is at the helm. Or perhaps a new "secret" recipe is being tried out on the clientele. In any case, give the place a chance and try it again.

It wouldn't be in this book if it wasn't great at least twice for these two veteran Bloody drinkers. Variables do occur, and one must always give an establishment a second chance. Do not judge the drink by poor service, an unhappy bartender, or bad timing all the way around. . . . Sit back and enjoy the drink! And don't forget to ask if that Bloody comes with a beer chaser!

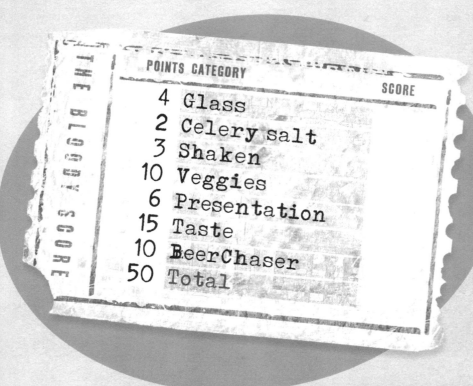

THE BLOODY SCORE

POINTS CATEGORY	SCORE
4 Glass	
2 Celery salt	
3 Shaken	
10 Veggies	
6 Presentation	
15 Taste	
10 BeerChaser	
50 Total	

SOBELMAN'S
PUB & GRILL MILWAUKEE

Owners, Dave and Melanie Sobelman, met in 1993 at a restaurant where Melanie was Dave's waitress. Six years later and married with children, they purchased one of Milwaukee's original Schlitz taverns, located on St. Paul Avenue. The Joseph Schlitz Tavern was built by the brewery in 1889

during Prohibition and was allowed by law to sell their beer. When the couple purchased the bar, it had jars of pickled products from Bay View Packing, which was still located right next door. There were pickled pigs' feet, pickled eggs, pickled onions . . . you name it! Dave thought about how he could incorporate all of this pickled produce into a scrumptious and unique drink . . . and what other drink than a Bloody Mary would do all of it justice?

Sobelman's Bloody Mary is served in a 14-ounce mason jar and comes with an 8-ounce Miller Lite chaser. . . FREE OF CHARGE! Dave doesn't skimp on the veggies either! This Bloody Mary is an appetizer in and of itself. Included in this snack in a glass is: a brussels sprout, a cube of cheddar cheese, a sausage stick, a celery stalk, a scallion, a pickled onion, a green olive, a cherry tomato, a pickle, a mushroom, a lemon slice, a shrimp, AND a mini-cheeseburger—bun and all!

THE BLOODY SCORE

THE BLOODY SCORE	POINTS CATEGORY	SCORE
	4 Glass	4
	2 Celery salt	0
	3 Shaken	0
	10 Veggies	10+2
	6 Presentation	6
	15 Taste	14
	10 BeerChaser	7
	50 Total	43

1900 W. ST. PAUL AVENUE
MILWAUKEE, WI 53202
414-931-1919
www.milwaukeesbestburgers.com

SobelmanS

Every bartender prepares your Bloody with gloves on! They use a "special mix" recipe given to Dave by a liquor salesman, and they usually serve 70-100 Bloody Marys each day and over 250 Bloodys on Saturdays! Enjoy!

But leave room for one of their Chicken Sobelman sandwiches or one of their famous burgers, like the Sobelman or the Loser Burger (That's another story entirely. . . . Ask Dave about it when you're at the bar!)

Don't be concerned if the place is crowded. Even though they recently built an addition that seats 48-50 people, you may still have to wait. And when the weather is inviting, there's plenty of outdoor seating. This is a very popular spot at any time of day. But, no worries, Dave's there 24/7 making sure everyone is happy! Be patient. . . . It is worth the wait.

THE WICKED HOP

MILWAUKEE

The Wicked Hop is located in the oldest building in Milwaukee's Historic Third Ward, the turn-of-the-century warehouse and manufacturing district and now the hot spot for galleries, boutiques, designer studios, and restaurants. The Merchant Mills building, where The Wicked Hop resides, was built in 1875 on what was known as Commission Row.

This block of buildings housed warehouses, fruit vendors, and other merchants. According to co-owner Miles O'Neil, his space was also used as a photo studio in the 1990s. He opened the bar and restaurant, along with his step-brother Andrew in April 2004.

"Wicked hop" is a baseball term for a ball that spins and bounces off the dirt, making it nearly impossible to catch. "Wicked hop" could also be a term used when you've had one too many beers!

THE BLOODY SCORE

POINTS	CATEGORY	SCORE
4	Glass	4
2	Celery salt	0
3	Shaken	2
10	Veggies	10+2
6	Presentation	5
15	Taste	14
10	BeerChaser	8
50	Total	45

The Cream City Brick interior walls of the bar and restaurant are decorated with photographs of Wisconsin-born actors. But the real attraction is their Bloody Mary ... voted Milwaukee's Best Bloody Mary in 2013 by readers at www.onmilwaukee.com and The Shepherd Express. Miles attributes this honor to a "house-special" formula that is mixed in 12-15 gallon containers, kept cold, and stirred all day long to maintain taste consistency! The secret ingredients include horseradish and TABASCO® Sauce, making this a very spicy Bloody.

**345 N. BROADWAY
MILWAUKEE, WI 53202
414-223-0345**
www.thewickedhop.com

The Wicked Hop serves a 16-ounce Bloody Mary, but if you want to have even more fun, try the 96.628-ounce Glass Slipper! It has all the same delicious ingredients, only MORE of them! It is served in a plastic German beer boot that you get to take with you when you finish (if you can)!

What makes this Bloody one of the best is the mini snack that tops it! It includes: a green olive, a peeled shrimp, a beef stick, a Walnut Street portabella mushroom, a Milwaukee's Midget Kosher Pickle, the obligatory lemon and lime slices, and those incredible mozzarella whips! These long pieces of string cheese wind around the top of the glass, creating a mountain of cheese! Yum! A 5-ounce Riverwest Stein chaser makes this Bloody bloody good!

There is a rich history to the Horse and Plow Bar and Restaurant. This historic tavern was constructed in 1924 as a recreation center and tap room for Kohler Co. workers who lived at The American Club. Dedicated on June 23, 1918, The American Club had a significant place in the development of Kohler Co. and Kohler Village. This example of a visionary concept of humanitarian interest in the worker can be contributed to Walter J. Kohler, Sr., during his tenure as president of Kohler Co. from 1905 to 1940. Kohler Co. is the worldwide leader in plumbing products and is still situated in the heart of the Kohler community.

THE BLOODY SCORE

POINTS	CATEGORY	SCORE
4	Glass	4
2	Celery salt	0
3	Shaken	3
10	Veggies	10+2
6	Presentation	4
15	Taste	12
10	BeerChaser	5+2
50	Total	42

But, enough history. The real reason this establishment has been included in the Best Bloody list is due to their fantastic Bloody Mary. This Bloody is 16 ounces of made-to-order spicy goodness. One of their top bartenders will add horseradish on demand—or anything else for that matter! If it is not to your liking, she will start all over ... but that won't happen, especially when you sample the mini salad bar expertly arranged on top! Named by Chef and Restaurant Manager

44 HIGHLAND DRIVE
KOHLER, WI 53044
920-457-8888
www.americanclub.com
www.facebook.com/TheHorseandPlow

Loren Rue, this "Mary of a Meal" includes a large celery stalk, lemon and lime slices, a skewer with a pickle, a pickled onion, two green olives, two mushrooms, an asparagus spear, a jalapeño pepper, and a brussels sprout! All of this for only $5.00 on Sundays!

Although the chaser is complimentary, it is only a 4-ounce beer. However you do have the astounding choice of 19 BEERS ON TAP, ranging from ales imported from Belhaven, Scotland, and Belgium and boasting 11 local brews from Wisconsin, including a root beer! To help you with this decision, any of their outrageous barkeeps will let you taste test those as well.

Enjoy your brew while lounging in the relaxing ambiance of nostalgic photographs from days gone by. Rest your elbows on tabletops that are made from the original American Club bowling lanes, which were located in the building where the bar now exists. Now that's a bit of bloody history! Cheers!

HINTERLAND
BREWERY & RESTAURANT
GREEN BAY

Yes, Hinterland Brewery in Green Bay makes world-famous beer, but they also make infused vodkas as well. This top-10 Bloody Mary not only has a secret recipe mix (which includes mysterious seasonings like coriander, fennel, and sriracha ... shhhh!!!), but the barkeep also uses a variety of infused vodkas when mixing your drink ... his choice or yours! The "over-the-top" 20-ounce glass scores extra points in this book! And you get your choice of a beer chaser.

It just can't get any better, you say?
Well, it does!

THE BLOODY SCORE

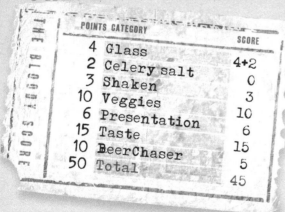

POINTS CATEGORY	SCORE
4 Glass	4+2
2 Celery salt	0
3 Shaken	3
10 Veggies	10
6 Presentation	6
15 Taste	15
10 BeerChaser	5
50 Total	45

Here's the list of veggies that top this tall, yummy Bloody:

- A deep fried goat cheese curd
- A house-made sausage, sliced thick
- A shrimp ceviche
- A mushroom
- Two olives
- Pickle
- And a lemon slice to make it pretty!

313 DOUSMAN STREET
GREEN BAY, WI 54303

920-438-8050

www.hinterlandbeer.com
www.facebook.com/HinterlandBrewery
@hinterlandbeer

The price might be a bit over the top at $13, but it is well worth the cost and the wait. I can just see the bartender creating each Bloody to perfection, as a chef prepares a meal. What a beautiful sight to see delivered to the table. The full-size beer adds to the glamour of the presentation. No complaints here! Maybe just one . . . after consuming the huge "salad" and drinking the yummy Bloody and beer, there's not much room for dinner! But one has to dig deep, because you can't miss out on the great menu offerings. Hinterland prides itself on serving its patrons contemporary American cuisine, creating dishes with bold flavors and uncommon pairings. The chefs have a relationship with small local growers and ranchers to provide customers with extraordinary game, hand-foraged mushrooms, and heirloom produce. They also work with fishermen from Honolulu, Seattle, and Portland, Maine, to bring fresh seafood in daily. Come on, you can do it! After all, it's Green Bay Packer territory, and everyone is a champion!

The atmosphere is elegant, yet comfortable. Dress up or dress down, but do dress. Nudity is frowned upon in Green Bay unless you happen to be at Lambeau Field during a Packer's home game! Then, by all means, do what you will! After the game, stop in at Hinterland to finish your day with a scrumptious Bloody Mary that beats all the rest! GO PACK GO!

Traveling south of Madison, touring the countryside, we came upon a little place called Kroghville . . . okay, just kidding! The innkeeper at the B&B we were staying at told us about this bar in the middle of nowhere that served a pretty darn good Bloody Mary . . . so we followed her directions and actually found the place. And it is an oasis! Friendly, happy people inside enjoying a football game, music, and oftentimes rowdy conversation! Live music every other Sunday adds to the atmosphere. From the outside, one would never guess the happening going on inside.

Kroghville was founded in the 1850s by Casper Krogh. He milled the wood found in this area used to construct artificial limbs for Civil War veterans. The home across the street from the Oasis was built by Casper Krogh, visited many times by Ulysses S. Grant, and is now the home of Oasis owner, Jeffrey Baumgartner. The Kroghville Oasis was the United States Post Office up until 1859. Some stories tell of the brothel that stood here as well. We're not asking any questions about that... We're here to enjoy the Bloody Mary!

Well, it is more than we bargained for! Jeffrey, the owner, bartender, and chef at the Oasis, makes a fantastic drink, and the veggies score a mighty 14!

THE BLOODY SCORE

	POINTS CATEGORY	SCORE
4	Glass	3
2	Celery salt	0
3	Shaken	0
10	Veggies	10+2
6	Presentation	6
15	Taste	12+2
10	BeerChaser	5
50	Total	42

N5942 COUNTY HIGHWAY O
WATERLOO, WI 53594
320-634-5321
www.facebook.com/kroghville-oasis

Here's the list:

- Cheese cube
- Slim Jim
- Green pepper
- Radish
- Carrot
- Pickle
- Celery
- Pepperoncini
- Asparagus
- Green bean
- Two onions
- Mushroom
- Green olive
- Black olive
- Jalepeño

WOW! It is really a salad in a glass! And to top it all off, he provides a bucket of seasonings with each serving—13 different brands of seasonings to add to your Bloody at your own discretion.

On Sundays, Jeffrey serves 25-cent chicken wings from 10 to 2 p.m. And they are delicious, just like everything else at the Kroghville Oasis! This place may be out in the boonies, but it is a worthwhile trip! Easiest way to find this happening place is to take Hwy 94 West to Hwy 73; take a left onto Cty Rd BB, then a right on Cty Rd. O. It's just 15 miles east of Madison, and you will love the scenery along the way! Enjoy the ride!

WEARY TRAVELER FREEHOUSE

Walking into Weary Traveler Freehouse located on the legendary Williamson Street (Willy Street) in Madison, you are immediately enveloped with warmth and great scents coming from the kitchen. The wood floors and walls, mismatched chairs, and crazy artwork create a hipster atmosphere that you can't ignore. The laid-back environment is warm and inviting, and the stack of board games on the wall ensures that you will stay awhile as you savor the great food, including their famous Bad-Breath Burger and their yummy, spicy Bloody Mary. Co-owner Bregan and his staff make the secret recipe for the mix. It definitely has horseradish, but what else? Not sure, but it is a good Bloody, earning it, at its best, a 41 out of 50.

THE BLOODY SCORE

POINTS CATEGORY	SCORE
4 Glass	4
2 Celery salt	2
3 Shaken	1
10 Veggies	8
6 Presentation	5
15 Taste	13
10 BeerChaser	8
50 Total	41

Included with the Bloody are garnishments of green olive, mushroom, brussels sprout, onion, pickle, and the usual lemon slice. The beer chaser comes with your choice of any of their 8 beers on tap ... even a port or Guinness! Bonus!

After a long day walking up and down Willy Street visiting the eclectic shops only Madison has to offer, stop in at the Freehouse; you will not be disappointed. Oh, and the name "Freehouse" means that the establishment is not tied to a brewery, as many of them were in 18th-

1201 WILLIAMSON STREET
MADISON, WI 53703
608-442-6207
www.wearytravelerfreehouse.com

WEARY TRAVELER

century London. Those pubs were actually owned by the brewery and were contracted to buy the beer from the brewery! Not the case at Weary Traveler. You will find a plethora of brews by the bottle or on tap! Don't you just love freedom?!

Besides the food, drinks, and board games available at Weary Traveler, you can enjoy the mixed group of patrons here at all times of the day. Everyone is friendly, including the staff! You can eavesdrop on some fascinating conversations or start one of your own! All topics are open for discussion.

At the Weary, you'll feel right at home.

Side note: In 1836, James Doty named his imaginary city after Former President James Madison, principal author of the U.S. Constitution. Doty named Madison's main streets after some of James Madison's colleagues from the summer of 1787 who had worked with him to frame the world's first blueprint for democracy. Williamson Street was named for Hugh Williamson of North Carolina, a licensed Presbyterian preacher and a professor of mathematics. As befits a preacher and academic, he served on several committees and argued often in the debates during the summer of 1787. (Hey, this is our state capital! There has to be some history lesson involved in this Bloody write-up!)

KITTY O'REILLYS IRISH PUB **STURGEON BAY**

What would a Bloody Mary book be without including a true Irish pub? It would be blarney without one! Yes, there are many Irish pubs in Wisconsin; in fact, there are just about as many pubs as there are Irish people on St. Patrick's Day! Kitty O'Reillys Irish Pub in Sturgeon Bay has all the Irish spirits, including Guinness, Kilkenny, and Smithwicks, traditional Irish food, and live traditional Irish folk music/jam sessions (you can join in if you bring your instrument!) on the first and third Wednesday of each month, year round! Most importantly, my dear lass or lad, it has a good ol' Irish Bloody Mary that includes a chaser you can choose yourself from 12 different brews!

Yes, I can say it is an Irish Bloody Mary, because after the mix is poured into the 20-ounce goblet of ice, it is topped off

THE BLOODY SCORE

POINTS	CATEGORY	SCORE
4	Glass	4+1
2	Celery salt	1
3	Shaken	2
10	Veggies	10+1
6	Presentation	6
15	Taste	13
10	BeerChaser	6
50	Total	44

with a bit o' Guinness! The pickled veggies are great too and come with a Klement's Sausage and lots o' Renard's Mozzarella Whips layered on the top of the glass!

**59 E. OAK STREET
STURGEON BAY, WI 54235**

920-743-7441

www.kittyoreillys.com
kittyoreillys@gmail.com
@kittyoreillys

I must say that, even though we were enjoying our snacks in a glass, we just had to order some food from their great menu, which includes a Kilt Tilter Wrap, Irish Stew, Corned Beef and Hash, and Kitty's Cheeseburger topped with potato fries! O' yeah! All good!

Voted the "Best Happy Hour in Door County," Kitty O'Reillys offers drink specials every night along with 25-cent wings or $1 tacos or burgers, depending on the night. On Sundays, their Kitty's Loaded Bloody Mary is only $5.00! Of course, during Packer games, they provide free Jell-O shots every time the Packers score a touchdown! Go Green and Gold!

In true Irish tradition, Kitty O'Reillys website has a "Countdown to St. Patrick's Day" clock that counts down the seconds to next year's festivities. But with everything Irish they have to offer, every day at Kitty's is St. Patrick's Day. Their slogan is "Great Food, Great People, Great Spirits, Great Fun!" So go on in and join the fun! You don't have to be Irish to love this place!

BERNIE'S PUB/
SCHREINER'S RESTAURANT
FOND DU LAC

This landmark restaurant just off Hwy 41 in Fond du Lac is well known to many travelers around the country. Established in 1938 on North Main Street by Albert and Regina Schreiner, the restaurant is famous for its delectable, nutritious, and traditional meals, such as baked chicken and mashed potatoes, sausage and German potato salad, and liver and onions. Their daily list of fresh-baked pies, such as pumpkin, walnut, and sour cream raisin, makes it difficult to decide which one to buy.

Today, Schreiner's Restaurant is recognized as one of the busiest and most successful restaurants in Wisconsin. One hundred skilled employees serve breakfast, lunch, and dinner to an average of 1700 guests per day, or 600,000 per year.

THE BLOODY SCORE

	POINTS	CATEGORY	SCORE
	4	Glass	4
	2	Celery salt	2+1
	3	Shaken	0
	10	Veggies	7
	6	Presentation	4
	15	Taste	12
	10	BeerChaser	10
	50	Total	40

More on the history of this fine establishment is available at www.fdlchowder.com/history for those of you interested in that sort of thing.

Bernie's Pub was built by a local interior design firm for Schreiner's in honor of the owner's son, Bernie Schreiner, who inherited the place in 1971. A cozy, friendly pub, Bernie's serves a wonderful Bloody Mary using a standard Bloody Mary mix. The addition of Worcestershire sauce, TABASCO® Sauce, and (get this) A.1.® Steak Sauce makes this Bloody

taste darn good! The veggies rate pretty high too, with three mushrooms and two olives along with a giant pickle. But what really makes this Bloody stand out is the Rhinelander Shorty that accompanies it—7 ounces of the fine brew made right in Wisconsin. Bernie's Pub boasts monthly beer and martini specials and has a Pub Grub menu of its own that includes a delicious BBQ pork slider.

After enjoying a delicious meal and a fantastic Bloody Mary at Bernie's Pub/Schreiner's Restaurant, take a leisurely drive through downtown Fond du Lac. Its quaint Main Street with many unique and locally-owned shops will certainly delight you! When you get thirsty, Fond du Lac does have a number of Bloody Marys that taste great but just don't meet our strict criteria. Stop in at Oscar's, Backyard Bar and Grill, Irish's, Ala Roma, or O'davey's for tasty, thirst-quenching Bloodys. Each one is delicious and deserves mention here. Maybe we are a bit biased, but Fond du Lac does know how to serve a great Bloody Mary and always that important FREE beer chaser! If Fond du Lac gets on the map for anything, it will be that you don't have to drive too far between bars to find a good Bloody Mary!

BLUEPHIES
RESTAURANT& VODKATORIUM
MADISON

Bluephies is not just a great restaurant with a varied menu, it is a VODKATORIUM! Add that to your Funk & Wagnalls! The owners have created a variety of vodkas infused with bacon or jalapeño or pineapple or sage or, well, you get the idea! There is an entire page of vodkas available all the time with a long list of martinis and liquid desserts! Their "mantinis" pack more of a punch for those who love their vodka more than they love anything else!

But let's get to their Bloody Mary! They serve a standard Bloody Mary made with Zing Zang™ and garnished with celery and olives; a chipotle-infused vodka Bloody with the additional jalapeño-stuffed olives and a dash of Sriracha; a Bloody Maria made with tequila; and our favorite, the FAT BOY Bloody Mary. This one tops them all. It is made with their house-made bacon-infused vodka, spiced tomato

THE BLOODY SCORE

POINTS	CATEGORY	SCORE
4	Glass	4
2	Celery salt	2
3	Shaken	0
10	Veggies	10+2
6	Presentation	6
15	Taste	13
10	BeerChaser	4
50	Total	41

juice (Zing Zang™), one large string cheese stick, asparagus, celery, two pickled mushrooms, an onion, two jalapeño-stuffed olives, and a thick slab or two of crispy bacon! Oh my! The beer chaser will cost you a buck, but, hey, get over it! This is a darn good—no, great—Bloody Mary!

2701 MONROE STREET
MADISON, WI 53703
608-231-3663
www.bluephies.com

Bluephies
restaurant & vodkatorium

One last note:
If you just cannot decide which Bloody to try, you can order a Bloody
Mary Flight . . . a trio of 8-ounce Bloodys! Or how about breakfast in
a glass? Their Wakey Wakey Eggs and Bakey Bloody Mary serves up a
GIANT ol' scotch egg (boiled egg wrapped in sausage, then breaded and
deep fried), bacon, lemon, lime, olives, and string cheese put on top of a
house-infused bacon vodka Bloody Mary with Zing Zang™ and a bit of
Fuel Café stout beer! Served from 8 a.m. to 2 p.m. only on Saturdays and
Sundays. Good Morning, Sunshine!

Bluephies offers contemporary food in an ultra-modern atmosphere,
and they are open 7 days a week! It's a busy place, so reservations are
encouraged, especially on Saturdays and Sundays when they serve
brunch. We only waited 30 minutes, but who knew? We were at the bar
enjoying our FAT BOY Bloody Mary appetizer! So grab your coat, the
spouse, and the kids (they have a kiddie menu that does not include
vodka), and get yourself to Bluephies! Their slogan is "We're serious
about fun food." And
we believe
them!

INDUSTRI CAFÉ

MILWAUKEE

I know this may seem strange to say, but there is a Bloody Mary War going on in Milwaukee! Sobelman's and Wicked Hop are already listed in this book with their amazing Bloodys, but it has to be mentioned that Benelux, Trocadero's, AJ Bombers, and Triskele's also have tasty Bloodys as well.

However there is one venue that has gone way out of the box to present a magical Bloody Mary that definitely competes with the rest and deserves recognition here. The Bloody at INdustri Café is fantastic! As their website states, "INdustri features classic dishes in the New American Style. Our focus is on technique and freshness, while delivering the highest quality product at a reasonable price. We proudly support Wisconsin and everything local." I must agree! Their food is wonderful, and their Bloody Mary is an extension of the quality of their products and their overall style of presentation.

THE BLOODY SCORE

POINTS	CATEGORY	SCORE
4	Glass	4+1
2	Celery salt	0
3	Shaken	3
10	Veggies	10+2
6	Presentation	5
15	Taste	14
10	BeerChaser	6
50	Total	45

The café itself is a symbol for what the two owners stand for, paying homage to Milwaukee-based industries: agriculture, artists, manufacturing, and the service industry itself. There is a lack of a stringent dress code, so the wait staff is able to express their own personal (and oftentimes that means a bit outrageous . . . but all wonderfully acceptable) style.

There are works from local artists on the Cream City Brick walls, and a local liquor menu with a beer list that only includes Wisconsin-based products. The use of a local farm-to-table coop makes INdustri Café uniquely different from all other restaurants in the area.

What does all this mean for the Bloody Mary drinker, you might ask? Well, these local ingredients make a tasty, almost-perfect mix that compliments the outrageous appetizer sitting on top of a 24-ounce oversized glass!

524 SOUTH 2ND STREET
MILWAUKEE, WI 53204
414-224-7777
www.industricafe.com

INdustri
CAFÉ

The use of the local Great Lake Distillery's Rehorst Vodka to make their in-house infused vodka with roasted poblanos, red onions, and many other mysteriously wonderful ingredients adds a unique flavor to this amazing drink. The in-house and locally pickled veggies get a higher-than-standard rating due to the large grilled prawn that rests between two sausage sticks, two olives, two mushrooms, an onion, brussels sprout, pepper, asparagus, pickle, celery stalk, and two fresh cheese curds from Clock Shadow Creamery. Add your traditional lime and lemon slices, and Voila! If you can handle all of that and still order a meal, congratulations! You will enjoy every bit of this Bloody and appreciate that every ingredient is locally produced!

Yes, there is a Bloody Mary war going on, but this war is to our advantage, Bloody Mary Drinkers! We get to enjoy every one of these Milwaukee Bloodys and decide for ourselves who the winner is! I think you will agree that we are all winners in this war! So go out there and enjoy the battle, but be safe and watch out for the other guy. You never know where another great Milwaukee Bloody Mary may arise to attack with all their best veggies and spicy homemade mix to conquer the world (of Bloody Marys, that is)!

Okay, call me crazy, but I just HAVE to include an 11th Best Bloody Mary in this guide. Yes, these Bloodys are only served on the 1st Sunday of each month, but they are **over the top!**

Barkeep and creative mastermind behind these spectacular Bloody Marys, Sarah Jayne Pickart, shops for all local ingredients, designs, and prepares these Bloodys for the patrons at O'davey's Pub. She usually serves over 150 of them on 1st Sundays with owner, Jessica Koepke, helping out behind the bar. I had the chance to admire and taste her "Wisconsinite Delight" Bloody Mary, and here is exactly what she created for this 18-inch-high dynamite of a drink:

- Bison Burger with bacon, cheddar cheese, lettuce, tomato, red onion, and a special sauce
- Triple Decker Fish Sandwich with bluegill, perch, walleye, and tartar sauce.
- Prime Rib Sandwich with au jus, buttery garlic baby potatoes, onions, mushrooms, and asparagus.
- Baby Brat with onions, kraut, and Dusseldorf mustard
- A chicken wing
- Pork BBQ ribs
- Bacon-wrapped jalepeño popper (my favorite)
- A giant venison stick
- Bacon (that crispy awesome kind!)
- A cup of potato salad
- A cup of cole slaw
- Garlic-dill cheese curds
- Mozzarella cheese whips
- Pepperjack cheese cube
- Cranberry white cheddar cheese cube
- A small, but sweet, corn on the cob
- Rye bread slice with butter
- Beer Salami
- Carrots
- Cucumber
- Green Bean
- Radish
- Sugar Snap Peas
- Green Onion
- Green Bell Pepper
- Celery Stalk
- Broccoli
- Pickle
- Mushroom
- Brussels Sprout
- Garlic Olive
- Blue Cheese Olive
- Olive
- Pepperoncini
- Pickled Dilly Bean
- Grilled Asparagus
- Garlic Clove
- Onion
- Jalapeno
- Cauliflower
- Baby sweet corn garnish

And her mix is made from scratch with over 35 ingredients (including fresh herbs, broths, mustards, juices, sauces, spices, and seasonings) plus Kettle One Vodka. Sarah will add any kind of hot sauce for heat, if you really think you need it after all those garnishes!

The glass, presentation and taste, along with the above MEAL, gives this Bloody Mary a Bloody score of way over 50! I know…that's just not right… but IT IS!

36 FOURTH STREET
FOND DU LAC, WI 54935
www.facebook.com/odaveyspubKoepke

Mark your calendars for the 1ST Sunday of every month when her masterpiece Bloody Marys are served at a new location: The Oshkosh Country Club on Hwy 45 along beautiful Lake Winnebago. Open to the public at 11 a.m. for this special event, the Bloody Mary party takes place poolside in the summer and around the double bar inside during Packer season. Be prepared to stand in line— maybe for hours—to get your very own personally handcrafted Sarah Jayne 1st Sundays Bloody Mary. These are works of art, people! Well worth the wait!

O'davey's still serves Sarah's fabulous (regular, but not ordinary) Bloody Marys, including 13 veggies, every day of the week. Stop in any time and enjoy your meal in a glass!

Cheers to you, Sarah! You are the champion of Bloody Mary makers and I, for one, cannot wait to see your next creation.

THE BLOODY MAP

···· EASTERN WISCONSIN ····

1 SOBELMAN'S PUB & GRILL
Milwaukee

2 THE WICKED HOP
Milwaukee

3 THE HORSE & PLOW
Kohler

4 HINTERLAND
Green Bay

5 KROGHVILLE OASIS
Kroghville

6 WEARY TRAVELER
Madison

7 KITTY O'REILLYS
Sturgeon Bay

8 SCHREINER'S/BERNIE'S PU
Fond du Lac

9 BLUEPHIES
Madison

10 INDUSTRI CAFE
Milwaukee

11 O'DAVEY'S PUB
Fond du Lac

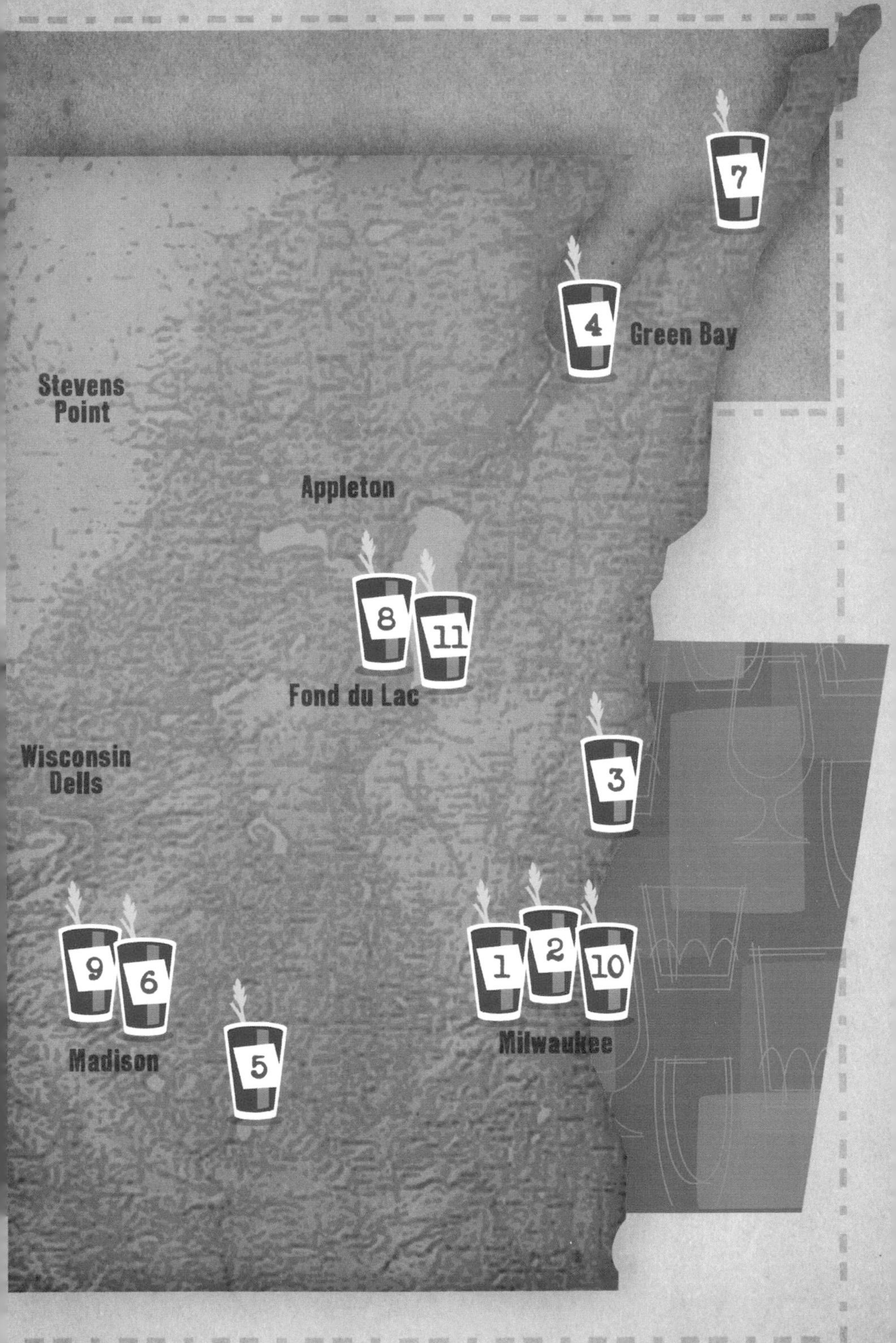

Stevens
Point

Green Bay

Appleton

Fond du Lac

Wisconsin
Dells

Madison

Milwaukee

MORE BLOODY INFORMATION

For the diet conscious, I have found this information:
An 8-ounce Bloody Mary is (according to the authors of Eat This, Not That!) "one of the few mixed drinks that actually offers some nutritional benefits. Made with low sodium V8, this drink offers a healthy dose of vitamins C, A, and lycopene, the cancer-fighting antioxidant found in tomatoes."

At 140 calories, 8 grams of carbs, and 150 mg of sodium, it is practically a health drink! There are many variations of the traditional Bloody Mary. According to information provided in Nancy Ross Ryan's column "LIQUID ASSETS 2000," here are some examples:

VIRGIN MARY Omit the vodka.

BLOODY MARIA Substitute tequila for vodka.

BLOODY MARY PEPPAR substitute pepper-flavored vodka for plain.

DANISH MARY Substitute Aquavit for vodka.

CALCUTTA MARY Add ½ teaspoon curry powder and a pinch of ground coriander.

SEASIDE MARY Use clam juice or Clamato©.

LONDON MARY Substitute gin for vodka.

BLOODY MARY QUITE CONTRARY Substitute sake for vodka.

CUBAN MARY Substitute white or light rum for vodka.

ITALIAN MARY Substitute grappa for vodka.

There are probably a bunch more . . . and homemade substitutions as well. There is a Bloody Mary for everyone, but this book rates the traditional Bloody Mary using vodka chosen by the bartender.

If you have a favorite variation of the Bloody, send your ideas to info@thebloodytrail.com, and I'll add it to the list!

THE BLOODY END?

The eleven establishments listed in this guide are only the beginning!
The search continues, and you can be a part of it! Remember to use the
postcards included with the book or send one of your own design to:

The Bloody Trail
P.O. Box 132
Fond du Lac, WI 54936-0132

Or go to www.thebloodytrail.com to register your favorites. If I agree with
you, your name and recommendation will appear in the next volume.

Enjoy the bloody journey, but remember, DON'T DRINK & DRIVE!
Always take a designated driver with you so you can thoroughly enjoy
The Bloody Trail.

BIBLIOGRAPHY

www.wikipedia.org

www.BestBloodyMary.com

Joseph Scott and Donald Bain, The World's Best Bartender's Guide, HP Books 1998.

Eat This, Not That! by David Zinczenko, Editor-in-Chief of Men'sHealth; with Matt Goulding; Rodale Publishers, ©2008.

Nancy Ross Ryan, article: LIQUID ASSETS 2000, www.twofresh-twofold.com

BAR / RESTAURANT & LOCATION

_____

COMMENTS

_____

_____

_____

_____

_____

_____

_____

_____

THE BLOODY SCORE

POINTS	CATEGORY	SCORE
4	Glass	
2	Celery salt	
3	Shaken	
10	Veggies	
6	Presentation	
15	Taste	
10	BeerChaser	
50	Total	

BAR / RESTAURANT & LOCATION

_____

COMMENTS

_____

_____

_____

_____

_____

_____

_____

_____

THE BLOODY SCORE

POINTS	CATEGORY	SCORE
4	Glass	
2	Celery salt	
3	Shaken	
10	Veggies	
6	Presentation	
15	Taste	
10	BeerChaser	
50	Total	

KEEP TRACK OF YOUR OWN BLOODYS HERE!
Score your finds and save 'em for future reference

BAR / RESTAURANT & LOCATION

COMMENTS

POINTS	CATEGORY	SCORE
4	Glass	
2	Celery salt	
3	Shaken	
10	Veggies	
6	Presentation	
15	Taste	
10	BeerChaser	
50	Total	

BAR / RESTAURANT & LOCATION

COMMENTS

POINTS	CATEGORY	SCORE
4	Glass	
2	Celery salt	
3	Shaken	
10	Veggies	
6	Presentation	
15	Taste	
10	BeerChaser	
50	Total	

KEEP TRACK OF YOUR OWN BLOODYS HERE!

Score your finds and save 'em for future reference

BAR / RESTAURANT & LOCATION

COMMENTS

THE BLOODY SCORE

POINTS	CATEGORY	SCORE
4	Glass	
2	Celery salt	
3	Shaken	
10	Veggies	
6	Presentation	
15	Taste	
10	BeerChaser	
50	Total	

BAR / RESTAURANT & LOCATION

COMMENTS

THE BLOODY SCORE

POINTS	CATEGORY	SCORE
4	Glass	
2	Celery salt	
3	Shaken	
10	Veggies	
6	Presentation	
15	Taste	
10	BeerChaser	
50	Total	

THE BLOODY SCORE

KEEP TRACK OF YOUR OWN BLOODYS HERE!
Score your finds and save 'em for future reference

BAR / RESTAURANT & LOCATION

_____

COMMENTS

POINTS	CATEGORY	SCORE
4	Glass	
2	Celery salt	
3	Shaken	
10	Veggies	
6	Presentation	
15	Taste	
10	BeerChaser	
50	Total	

BAR / RESTAURANT & LOCATION

_____

COMMENTS

POINTS	CATEGORY	SCORE
4	Glass	
2	Celery salt	
3	Shaken	
10	Veggies	
6	Presentation	
15	Taste	
10	BeerChaser	
50	Total